CW00405158

glean

patrick james errington

ignitionpress

For my mum, dad, & brother

First published in 2018
by **ignition**press
Oxford Brookes Poetry Centre
Oxford Brookes University
OX3 0BP

© Patrick James Errington 2018

Cover design: Flora Hands, Carline Creative
Page design: Thomas Nicolaou

A CIP record for this book is available from the British Library

ISBN 978-1-9997412-2-8

Contents

If it must
be winter, let it be absolutely winter.

Linda Gregg

In the Event of Winter

If you look close, everything moves. But it's not enough.
The party winds down around you, your ears humming

to replenish the voices that have turned back, atoms of air
taking their cues from the cars on a wet street three stories

below. Tell yourself there's sometimes quiet. You are still
in the wild of your life, senses bringing news of winter

and departing. There's a glass of water in front of you, ringing
the table, gathering all too quick the warmth from your palm.

Each particle furiously staunching another. Consider
that waxwings wake in the cold. It is not enough to take

place. An event of viridian in the grass. There's no keeping
us together. Your body packs the wound it makes in the grey

field as you walk toward home. Though the door closes
behind you, another day bleeds itself dry across the snow.

On Highway 2A Near Blackfalds,
Alberta, as Night Comes On

You could come here and never arrive.
These towns like the memories of towns,
all flecks of colour, barn-reds and brown
sinking into the haze of greys that no one

no matter how hard they try can quite draw
a word for (as if any word could draw it
like the bodies they drew from the almost-
iced-over river dripping up the bank

to be dried, identified, packed away).
You could leave, have left, and still wake
with water in your mouth, water instead
of a name. Each town's name peeling slowly

off sheet-metal siding or a rust-graffitied
bridge, as though picked at by the passing
vacant stares of commuters hurtling down
the 2A to the city. There can be no tense

imperfect enough for this. In every distance,
grain silos stand through the snow like steel
slivers of history that catch on the little light.
Like cracked teeth after a fight. Your tongue

will never rub them smooth. I'm not sure
you'd ever want to. But then again, I'm not
you (and you're welcome). Maybe though
you wouldn't mind – maybe just this once

you can let yourself off the hook, let someone else feel a way across your life, just once.
The girl behind the bar winces as she cuts
her palm on a nick in the old wood surface.

She smiles at you, briefly, from deep beneath
her face as she folds her bleeding hand
in a rag. Her blood is a dark hole in the ice
on a river we were all so sure we could skate on.

Little Lit

So you break into another night without winter,
slipping inside the fabric of some hand-me-down

body. Beside you, you can sense the mass of your life,
its haunches bulked against you, its hide coarse

in your mouth. You have nothing
                                    to say. As you lead
it down the hall by a horn, feet sticking to hardwood,

little light scattered like broke china across the moteless,
motionless space, you scrawl your senses over the picture

frames, the measureless dark of small bedrooms, stuccoed
skies. Listen to a round snap of hooves that trails you,

until you step free onto the outgrown lawn, relishing
the gasp of frost in the webbing of your toes. But still,

the moon comes muffled by the streetlamps that buzz

in their glass hives, drooling honey. Your breath scrapes,
fogging the cold like starlings, you imagine, school

up from the pitch of a hawk. You consider how years of
quiet hold you together like a mould you never fill, still

wondering at the depths beneath the crests of houses
around you. Seas, you decide, as you turn back to yours,

follow the two sets of prints, sense the door closing
fast above you, fitting its frame, flawed, not like water.

Yew: Directive

Give it time and testament.

This living never fit—plumb
within your body, between

the platelets,
            the bone. Wear
life like a habit you can't

slip, quick-   bitten nail. Curl
into the cave your body carves,

the here in where you are. Plant
yourself,   grow

beyond your breath, feel out
the soil of you. This is hardly

breaking down or breaking
in. Feel another evening   broken

like a wave
                along your senses,
the chill of grass ruined across

your fingertip. You need know
nothing   of structure to learn

this breaking into leaf. Come.

I've tilled the clay with my
foreign tongue. Split open

your mouth like a shell. Let
your longest branches out.

White Lies

Say the quiet grows around you, that the slip of light
is all that pins my hand to your chest when the senses quit
taking and start offering up the little blueabout, the little
stones they've culled from the riverbed. Say you're always

> *You, and a river's deepest turns promising your body*
> *a new shape, a way down. Orphan of water,*
> *step back onto the bent rocks, into*
> *the warming of me. There's too much sky,*
> *too much breathing to be done. You say I've never been*

small in the smallest room. Say sea. Say it backward
in my ear. Or instead say there's nothing left but
the nest of rust, that your body is emptied of you - how
wide your eyes say you can say everything, wildly, out,

> *wrong enough to be forgiven or even to ask. Yet I bend,*
> *each night, to the sink as if to a nurse's hand,*
> *wait for the drought to wash me*
> *against the mirror. While you sleep, sometimes, I kneel*
> *on the cool tiles, hope they're white enough to take me in,*

like a Chinook arch of thunderhead, hurling itself
against a field of bent gold, of canola flowers and tar,
until at night it admits stars. Or like a deer, god-split
on the snow, giving out a language of paling clouds,

> *snow might come, but not without a break or a body*
> *to collect against. If I could invent a word for a blank*
> *square of my wall, would that make it real?*
> *It can't exist, white, you told me. I've seen snow only*
> *from the shadows, said you by saying everything you are not,*

its marrow sucked from the open ulna until it draws
crystals of cold to the muzzle. Say you said
it all, your colours to the coils of your fingerpads,
what would you let light? Finches. Copper wire. Rome.
Caraway. You. Say this never happened.

Theorette of Relativity

How sour sweet music is,
When time is broke and no proportion kept!
William Shakespeare, Richard II

As for time and distance, there's evidence
tangled in the tuck and cluster of follicles
at the nape. Owls proportioned by a seething
static of feathers over something's torn body.
Measure only assumed in what keeps
time. Roots clutch to gauge their growth,
new shoots spun of larchwood. And as for
the hiss and shoal of rain – will nothing keep
from running? Is there a small portion of lynx
still shored by the islanded thicket? Some cells
I've heard are not shed, all your life, from
the crystal behind your iris if only to confirm
that your old house is somewhere beneath
the highrise. I, in the dusk, gather a last blade
of honey to be counted on my ribs. I'm dying
to prove just how much I've been alive.

Line of Best Fit

You see, I've been trying to put each thing back
into place. Like after the curtains on a shoebox

symphony finally close, and the old shadows
nose out from the den of our bare feet as we

hang, one by one, the streetlamp patterns back
on the walls like maps. I'm there in the dark

between countries, the dry field dry as my throat
and I'm digging. I feel like I'm always digging,

rooting my fingers in the frozen earth as if I
could hold me in this place through the swailing

that is to come. That has to come. It's making
a place for winter. That's what you tell me

every time the fire pries you open, plants its hot
promise beneath your tongue. But winter lives

in me already like a small creature, and I haven't
a heart to scare it up. And all the while hoarfrost

writes refusals in the dirt and still I'm digging
down between my lips for the cold cowered

in my teeth, and I haven't time, haven't light

left for scraping up the tufts of grist, fistfuls,
furrows—all these deaths fit to me, little plots

of dusk between the stalks—and nearly dark
now, a wild wind licking up the fire in my mouth

and I'm speaking, tongue splitting sparks from
a song I can't name, Come in, it goes, we sing.

Taxidermy in Burning House

Above all, he is careful. Unlacing the body,
a twine   white and patient as paper.

A process of exchange, a structure of one
for another, motion for motion, transaction.

In the cradle behind the ribs,   he plays
the horologist, unwinding the mechanisms,

the decay. He lines the vaulted organs, meticulous
as Murano glass, rasping out the rot. He has

always fancied himself a conservationist—But
he must work harder now, more quickly. The lung

next, the blood-sack economies depressed
beneath a haze of formalin. The heart-pocked

table is a scatter of excesses, indivisible
remainders. Wet boundaries of preservation

hardening. The glass begins to sweat, like—No,
there's no time left. The mouth, now—of course

the mouth, heaped beneath the face, shut
into an expression of averages. He sets the lips

for something,   no, not quite like speech.
Something harder, older. Feathers curl in the heat.

The eyes return each colour unused. Honey slips
between the sinews,   a reader returning one

last time. Loss finding a form it can keep.

Lessons in River Reading, 1997

Given time, everything smooths
into itself, the pull of your arms into
        the current, the shudder and grit
                in the sinew sloughing off. And
        as it should, you think, if you ever
do think about it, the thoughts
        rising like trout to dimple the surface
                at dusk with soft rain, or like a lick
        of white on a standing wave that marks,
beneath it, the careful heave of the riverbed.
        That's how your father taught you to read
                the river, in the soft serifs of eddies
and Os that trail your paddle along the gunwale.
        You've always loved the smoothness
                of that word, how it rolls loose in
        its letters, its syllables, like a cold stone
in your mouth, your tongue worrying
        at its broken places, like that tooth
                you chipped on a paddle blade
                when you were still learning what
        water can do when it breaks. The pain
of it still sticks jaggedly through the surface
        of your childhood, furrowing the features
                where all the rest of those days
        wear away into a scent of white pine
and dusk. You can barely remember
        your father saying—But your paddle
catches, twists off a rock and the boat
                pitches, sloshing meltwater over
        the gunwales and sharpening your breath
                before, calmly, the current, like
a hand you once knew well, rights you
        in the moment that carries on.

Inheritance

You've had that dream again. You know the one
        that wakes you. You rise to rough wood floors, doors

that only ever open in, whining away as if they could blame you
        for wanting to leave. But you're alive
                and can't help feeling

forgotten, somewhere in your body like a wreck in deep
        water. When you walk out to your car, the grey light is shot

with green and salt, your senses pressing so heavily
        around you it gets hard to breathe. And even the sky weighs

enough these days to crush the best of them. You sometimes
        hear what sounds
                like small bones splinter. Come on,

be reasonable, think it through. Yet it hurts every time you think of it,
        and of this unhorsed town no one really grows up in, the greys

and the one bar that every evening seems to lead to, like numbers
        on a clock that's always a little behind the time. Isn't this the life

you asked for? The hand-me-down that had looked so good on
        your big brother, worn thin
                over you now, thin over your shoulders,

your ribs like the empty substation your brother's friends haunted
        as kids, consecrating it with stolen beer and piss. But you made it

your temple, imagining how gods once hummed in the wiring,
        the rituals, the sacrifice. But even then you'd begun to find yourself

beneath your senses, your body just some house you inherited, never
        really yours. The taste of iron rusting
                in the synapse, the touch come

apart at the seam. You know there are people in foreign countries,
        their language reaching, right now, like a hand for your life,

their voices like rain along a windowpane, pooling on the sun-
        sealed dirt, the husks of wheat, the wind piled against

the baseboards. When the tv goes out, when the lights let slip
        their shadows, for a moment you can nearly
                feel someone. You wonder what,

if not you, will reach back when you wake in the dark. Who
        do you think you are?

Burning the Fields

Had I lain longer in the firebreak
of the senses. Had colour lingered,

patient, in the skin—already, the end
breeds beneath the bed, needles

out from the dark, veining the sheets
with a thin skein of frost. What animal

haunts the spelt, shivers
the broken stalks? Somewhere a lancet

of geese slits my chest like a skyline
bleeding winter.   Had I frayed

my teeth apart, made a nest in the down
of my mouth, would you have stayed?

Cold: Exchange

If I get anything from the lightless it's less
space, the senses all crowding in to touch
and breath. Right now in a plot of north

Canada, exposure alone is sufficient
to strip a drunk down to the body, but here
I'm frayed far from mine by the scrabble

of sheets on sleeplessness. Not much
as problems go, when people are dying
just outside my language, and try

as I might there are so many that elude
still the word for comfort as I stretch it
over the page like a hand, feel into the gut

beyond the human, groping down to dumb
mammal warmth. The distant country across
the mattress answers me in absence like

the quiet behind the door that yawns
for you: cold, it tells me, and I shiver out
from under a snow of sleep and no matter

how I churn, blink the frost from my eyes,
press my heart beyond me into things,
still this word, still this small word.

Still Life with Approaching Crow

There's nothing to distinguish
this from the last three-or-so
hundred fields they pass, but
for whatever reason they call it
far enough. The engine shaking
off its sound, voices dripping
from their mouths to the ground.
When they say let's go they won't
mean everyone, this time. Beyond,
a field frozen solid, expression-
less, stubbled with broken grain.
They'll leave him loose as teeth
in his life, lashed to a fencepost.
Blood gently unlacing the features
from his face and every wound
unwinding from its pain like wire.
It'll be days before anyone can tie
the term *missing* to what it has
to mean. The field and his flesh
grow significance against their will.

Kwashiorkor

Had I eaten my fill of you I might have lived.
The animals that take inheritance of me
would have gone hungry without any help,
bellies bloated for the lack. Might now
be baring too-bent bodies to the heaving sky
as it grinds through the pelts for the meat—
even the sun is starved round. Eating was a poor
relief, it seems. Because I did eat. I ate
everything: the whitewash off the walls down
to the baseboards. Chewed my elbows down
to the gristly joists, stuffed the eye with yarrow
to stop up the deserts sluicing out until all
I could see was veined red. Then ate root into
the dirt and lay there in the furrow looking up.
Had I sacrificed my little mammal hands
on a slab, would that have sated? Had I grown
greater on the sugars you hollowed would you
have stopped your offering? Had I slit myself
down the middle, let in the famished air, is there
something left in me that might fly out?

Half Measures

It's been years now since she left, and even
still he sleeps on just half the bed. After all,

it really is easier to make that way, quicker
to hide all evidence of dreaming, like photographs

hastily put back on the shelf. He's become
a tenant of fractioned closets, of half-portioned

recipes, of refracted light. He sometimes tells
himself, like time, there is managing in measure,

absence held in the hand-span, the half-heart,
the hair's breadth. For comfort, he remembers

seeing the great Dutch paintings – Dou, sometimes
Vermeer – the immeasurable lives made so nearly

bearable in the frame, slightness like a bird's
body in a plastic bag. As a child, he used to

count miles on telephone poles while, in front,
his parents spoke in weather-levelled voices.

When he'd told her this she pitied him. When
he would add up all the countries he wanted to

show her, she'd tell him that numbers are such
a man's way of holding the world, but, when

women love, they love innumerably. Softly,
he'd said he only wanted to hold her. He'd never

admit how, against her body, he felt so desperately
proportionate, how sometimes he would lie

along the bathroom tiles as though the seams
and scale would make him somehow bearable,

as a painting, would hold him. Not because
he needed holding, but maybe just to know loss

could be travelled, as he watched planes scrawl
across the unbound blue through the window.

So often, these days, he thinks of grief in terms
of distance. Carefully plotting out the lengths

involved in the longing, he imagines himself some
ancient philosopher slowly dividing the distance

toward home, thinking of a child's hands, still
sticky with the juice of a poorly-divvied fruit.

How impossibly small it all can seem, small
like distance, halved, and halved, and halved again.

Gleaning

On hands and knees, you take what you call
the middle ground. If a god can be found
here, it's because he couldn't commit either,

combing, like waves, the shingle, wanting
just some scrap worth settling on. Life,
at least, has settled on your body like silt

on that wreck no one survived. When
you, daily, wake, it's as if washed ashore.
When you wish, it's a hundred liferafts'

beacons swimming in the dark. Imagine
a language where these are no different.
You pray and it's enough. Instead you lie

awake, knotting sheets, small hours heaped
up like driftwood. You could manage, make
do, get by, and you can. But there's a loss

for every light, for every sense's salvage.
Just to be alive to this world is an act of war.
You know to take a hand, some small thing

will go unheld. Hands alone keep loss
from reclamation. Only in this language
is the sky something less than heaven.

To Be Redacted Should It Become Necessary

Winter again and, though it's early days yet, the sky and I
can sense its restraint. The old redactor's leaving work, stopping

in the shops on the corner to grab some bread, wine, whatever
is necessary. Milk, maybe – no need to reach for that one all

the way in back, everything will be drunk tonight – the last
of the autumn asters in a pail by the window. Take

only the things that are given. I could have loved you more,
I think. All those evenings, I held you as if I could hold you

together, like syntax. Your hair spilling loose. Past the bare
hotel kitchen, the dusk going soft what with all the gnawing

of dormice in the woodwork, the fallen thistle-seed sprouting
in the grass. A birdhouse empty and above. Even unkept, time

keeps us, years, like souvenirs, scraps brought back from some
well-planned holiday. Provence, maybe. Everything has a limit,

you used to say, the glimmer of city lights failing far below
against the gathering dark. I think of wisdom, now, not so much

as knowing or experience or regret. I could have loved you
through all hours, enough to slip ourselves loose from them like

numbering, like needing, and the poem might've ended here.
But I'm told the town's only editor slipped out early tonight

to buy asters, maybe because he knows there's really no use
staying to the end. Or maybe because there's someone waiting

back home, and it's been a long time, I gather, since he's done
something nice for her, something small and more than necessary.

To a Boyhood in Winter

What more
to say? What

of this snow
-rankled sky?

This low lie
of comfort, some

pale lip on these
car-furrowed streets

these towns strewn
with what should be

called living but
isn't. Even wolves

curl around their
rocking hearts

to sleep.
Eventually even

I will leave you
be as you ask.

Acknowledgements

Many thanks to the magazines, anthologies, and prizes in which versions of these poems have appeared: *The Adroit Journal, American Literary Review, Best New Poets, Boston Review, The Cincinnati Review, Cider Press Review, Contemporary Verse 2, Copper Nickel, Diagram*, the Flambard Poetry Prize, the McLellan Poetry Competition, *Sugared Water, West Branch* and the Wigtown Poetry Competition.

Epigraph is taken from Linda Gregg, 'Part of Me Wanting Everything to Live', in *The Sacraments of Desire* (Graywolf Press, 1991).

Thank you to all my many mentors, Bert Almon, Derek Walcott, Lucie Brock-Broido, Timothy Donnelly, Dorothea Lasky, Richard Howard, Alan Gilbert, Don Paterson, John Burnside, and to my dear friends, collaborators, co-conspirators at the University of Alberta, Columbia University, the University of St Andrews, back home, and abroad for your boundless support, guidance, and belief.

Thank you to everyone at **ignition**press for your trust in these poems and for giving them such a splendid home.